SEASON OF ANTICIPATING,
AN ADVENT DEVOTIONAL

BY
C.S.MCDONALD

SEASON OF ANTICIPATING, AN ADVENT DEVOTIONAL
Copyright © 2025 C. S. McDonald

Contents

Wishing you a

blessed Advent

J. McDonald

SEASON OF ANTICIPATING,

AN ADVENT DEVOTIONAL

A Gentle Reflection

Where is he? When will he return?
I know I've seen him.

I've seen him in the golden rays of the rising
sun shimmering over the newly fallen snow.

I've heard him in the rolling belly laugh of a
baby, in the quiet sigh of a sleeping puppy.

I've walked with him down a woodland path
as the leaves drift to the ground and the birds
sing their parting song.

Truly, he's been here all along drying tears,
calming fears, a quiet, gracious presence
swirling around me. Oh, what a glorious
comfort he is!

Yet we ask, when?
When will he return—especially now, in
this season of anticipating…this season of
Advent.

C.S. McDonald

DECEMBER 1ST

WHAT IS ADVENT?

WHAT DOES THE WORD ADVENT MEAN? It means waiting or anticipating the arrival of a person or an event. Advent is the glorious season, or four weeks, anticipating the birth of Christ and the preparation for his second coming.

Look around. There are so many things within church walls that celebrate Advent. In my church, one of the most beloved items is the Advent wreath. Our wreath sits upon a tall pedestal. Four candles are nestled in the wreath: Advent candles. Each week, we light one candle. In most churches, the colors of the candles are: one purple or blue candle and three pink candles.

I don't know about your congregation, but the children in ours are so excited during the lighting of each candle. The little ones are anticipating Christmas and the gifts they will receive. Indeed, Advent is an exciting season. Everyone is filled with anticipation.

So, how is the Advent wreath tied to Christmas, and what does it symbolize?

The wreath is formed in a circle. It has no beginning or end, symbolizing the eternity of God, the immortality of the soul, and the everlasting love and life we find in Christ. The wreath is made of evergreens, representing continuous life.

The candles are so beautiful amid the wreath, especially when all four are lit and the anticipating of Christmas is at its height. Each candle has a name and its own special connotation.

The first week of Advent, we light the purple or blue candle known as the Hope/Prophecy candle. This candle represents the hope and anticipation of the coming Messiah, who the prophets of the Old Testament foretold. The candle is a reminder that Christ's birth is the realization of the prophecies.

When the second week of Advent arrives, we light the first pink candle: the Peace/Bethlehem candle. This candle reminds us of Mary and Joseph's journey to Bethlehem and the peace Christ's birth brings.

Ah, the excitement is really starting to mount when the third week of Advent rolls around. The children can barely contain their anticipation when the Joy/Shepherd's candle burns brightly. This candle fills us with joy. It flickers with rejoicing as we anticipate the arrival of the Savior.

Our sanctuary is buzzing with gladness on week four and the last candle is lit. The Love/Angel's candle is a symbol of love. It represents God's love for all peoples and the angels' heralding peace on Earth! This candle fills us with the love and promise Christ's birth has brought into the world.

Advent...the beautiful season of anticipating the joy, love and the glory of our dear Savior, Jesus Christ's birth. Come, Lord Jesus!

PRAYER

Dearest Lord, we welcome the season of Advent,
rejoicing in our Savior, Jesus Christ.
We are filled with anticipation of the celebrations
and keeping Him close to our hearts and teaching
our children of his humble birth.
Thank you, Lord, for this season of anticipating, this
glorious season of Advent.

Amen.

DECEMBER 2ND

MATTHEW 11:15

LET ANYONE WITH EARS LISTEN!

ALONG A WINDING, WOODLAND TRAIL, or a busy shopping mall, gently whispering to a small child, *we're going this way*, gives the child a sense of reliable guidance from a loving parent. And it is that same guidance we, as adults, are in constant search of. Today's scripture points out to us the direction John the Baptist was offering the masses of his day—the path toward the coming Messiah, Jesus. John was sent ahead of Jesus to pave the way, heralding his arrival, encouraging all to follow his every step, and his every word.

Though, John was hardly whispering to be heard, Jesus's murmurs with tender cajoling in our ear, *come, we're going this way, my child.* Our Lord offers his comforting hand to lead us toward the Father. If we are listening, if we are focusing, Jesus is our travel companion through life's rocky pathways, our celebrations, and our consoler in times of despair.

During our lifetime, we may stray from Jesus's voice for more appealing endeavors. I know I have been guilty of such preoccupations: career, children's activities, social commitments. Ah, but Jesus is always waiting and ready to lead me. He whispers, *come, we're going this way, my child, then offers his hand*, and I return to the intended course of worship, prayer, study of the Lord's word, and fellowship. As God's son, Jesus paves the way for us as John did for him. We are so very blessed to have Jesus's hand on our shoulder leading us along the sometimes rough, sometimes joyful, and oftentimes solemn road. As in today's scripture, Let anyone with ears listen! The message may not sound quite the same as it did back then, still Jesus is urging us—*Come, we're going this way, my child.*

Prayer

Loving Lord, let Christ take my hand and lead me along the path you desire me to follow.

When life becomes busy or overwhelming, stay close with your comforting presence and your loving whisper, *Come, we're going this way.*

Amen.

December 3rd

Luke 3:10-11

And the crowds asked him, "What then should we do?" In reply he said to them, "Whoever has two coats must share with anyone who has none; and whoever has food must do likewise."

Ah, it truly is the most wonderful time of the year, isn't it? Advent. It is the time for family gatherings, singing those joyful Christmas hymns, and enjoying foods that are only baked during this magical season. Advent is also known for a time of giving. Generosity flows easily. Giving of ourselves seems almost effortless.

Churches of all denominations and many department stores display angel trees dangling with tags from local children and their Christmas wishes. Gift bags are loaded with toiletries and candy for the elderly in nursing facilities. And of course, the food pantries are stuffed to the brim with non-perishable foods for holiday meals. After all, it is Advent. Like the crowd gathered on the margin of the Jordan River, to be baptized and to hear John speak, we Christians ask, *"What then shall we do?"* We respond by collecting gifts for the children and the elderly and stacking the shelves in the food pantry. It is a satisfying feeling to give, and to be so charitable.

When John spoke to the crowd along the Jordan, there was no Advent season. No Christmas hymns, angel trees, nor food pantries. No. They came looking for repentance, and John told them of the Messiah yet to come, and how they needed to give of themselves. *"Whoever has two coats must share with anyone who has none; and whoever has food must do likewise."*

Truth be told, it's hard to give of ourselves. We lead busy lives. Advent is an amazing season, but what of the other seasons? Look around. Our world is rife with need. Compassion. Can we find a way to give of ourselves *all year*, during *all* the seasons? Even in the smallest of deeds?

Indeed, God is faithful and giving in all seasons.

Prayer

Gracious, loving Lord, help me find a path toward
giving of myself all year long.
Help me keep those in need close to my heart and
help where I can.
Keep your steady, guiding hand on my shoulder and
lead me in the direction you want me to go.
In Jesus's glorious name.

Amen.

DECEMBER 4TH

MARK 10:14-15

LET THE LITTLE CHILDREN COME TO ME; DO NOT STOP THEM. FOR IT IS TO SUCH AS THESE THE KINGDOM OF GOD BELONGS. TRULY I TELL YOU, WHOEVER DOES NOT RECEIVE THE KINGDOM OF GOD AS A LITTLE CHILD WILL NEVER ENTER IT.

BACK IN JESUS'S TIME, children were considered a disposable segment of society. In today's verse, Jesus was in a region of Judea, beyond the Jordan River. Crowds were gathering around him, and of course, he stopped to talk and teach them. Parents were bringing their little ones to Jesus; hopeful he would touch them or perhaps even smile at them.

I can imagine the children running toward him calling out, "Jesus! Jesus!" Maybe they were so delighted to see this amazing teacher they'd heard their parents speak of that they were all talking at the same time. In my mind, I can see our Lord smiling at them, laughing at their antics. Yet, the disciples were not so amused. They felt Jesus was there for one reason: to teach the people, not to waste his precious time on children.

The Gospel of Mark doesn't tell us exactly what the disciples were saying to the children, only that they spoke sternly to them. Now, it was Jesus who was not amused, and he rebuked them, *"Let the little children come to me; do not stop them."*

Jesus was trying to explain that we must have trust in God, as a child trusts and relies on their father. For God *is* our Father. Jesus's words, *whoever does not receive the kingdom of God as a little child will never enter it,* is a powerful message that we must place our trust in God and abandon our attitude of self-reliance and vanity that our accomplishments are of our own doing, or we can solve our problems without turning to the Father for help or guidance.

Furthermore, Jesus's admonishment of the disciples is another example that *everyone* is important in God's eyes; the weak, strong, poor, rich, sinners, and saints.

God wants us *all* to come to him with the trust, humility, and the faith of a child. After all, we *are* his children. We are dear to his heart, and his loving hand is *always* outstretched toward us.

PRAYER

Dearest Father in heaven, we know you are always there for us, and yet sometimes when we fall, we try to pick ourselves up without your help.
We toss in our beds with anxiety, and yet, you are just a whisper away.
Help us Father, help us to turn our heart to you.
Help us to reach for your hand and to grasp it, and know your love, compassion, and grace.
In Jesus's beautiful name.

Amen.

DECEMBER 5TH

PSALMS 23:5

YOU PREPARE A TABLE BEFORE ME IN THE PRESENCE OF MY
ENEMIES; YOU ANOINT MY HEAD WITH OIL; MY CUP OVER-
FLOWS.

WE DO NOT HAVE TO FACE OUR ENEMIES ALONE. God is
with us in the challenge of adversity. His protection and
comfort are draped around us as a shield. Who are our
enemies? A friend we have fallen out with? A family
member we can't seem to get along with? That office bully
we cannot find peace with, or can it be the bully cannot
find peace within themselves?

God wants us to find tranquility, but how do we
find it? He anoints our head, healing us from our grief,
and yes, the shiver of animosity we experience when our

antagonist is close. He urges us to forgive our enemies. Close our eyes and search our inner being to pardon our adversary. Forgiving is a hard task; a tall order, but it truly can be achieved. If we trust in God, his blessings and grace will help us find the strength to forgive and offer comfort, even when they are near.

Prayer

Dear Lord, delivery me from those who dislike me
or wish me harm.
Help me find the strength to forgive my enemies and
find comfort in your presence when they are near.

Amen.

A Gentle Reflection

An angel in disguise, you are.
Your intrinsic manner lifts our spirits,
even in our darkest moments.

Our God is ever so clever to bless us with
these beautiful souls whose eyes are filled
with pure love, compassion, and gratitude,
though I doubt we are deserving.

They nuzzle our cheek when it is stained with
tears.
They cannot speak, and yet their gentle gaze
whispers, I'm here.
They run and jump along the sylvan path
these angels of joy, prodding us to live in the
moment and to be thankful for everything
around us.

Everything in God's world.
God's secret angels—our God is a merciful,
kind God.

C.S. McDonald

DECEMBER 6TH

LUKE 2:10

THE ANGEL SAID TO THEM, "DO NOT BE AFRAID! FOR BE-
HOLD, I BRING YOU GOOD NEWS OF GREAT JOY THAT WILL
BE FOR ALL PEOPLE…"

ANGELS. THESE MYSTERIOUS, GLORIOUS BEINGS of God
are mentioned in the Bible two-hundred-eighty-five times.
They herald the news of the Messiah's birth to the lowly
shepherds in the fields. An angel is present at the tomb
of Jesus, announcing his resurrection to the women who
came to anoint his body with spices. They are constant
witnesses to the great triumphs and terrible failures of
God's people. Yet we are not given a solid description of
what an angel looks like.

People are fascinated by angels. Take a drive

through any neighborhood and you will undoubtedly see statues of angels in flower beds or among shrubbery. The statues are usually women with her heads bowed, hands clasped in prayer, and beautiful, full wings. Many people collect ceramic angels. Although they are usually more ornate than the garden statues, they are quite similar in appearance. Revelation 4:8 gives a rather disturbing depiction of angels: *And the four living creatures, each of them with six wings, are full of eyes all around and within…* this description sounds frightening, and not exactly the angels anyone wants in their garden or curio cabinet.

So, what do angels look like? What are angels? Many people believe in guardian angels, but do they really exist? Do angels walk among us, and if so, in what form?

Many years ago, I was at a friend's house while some relatives were visiting. I overheard an elderly aunt telling my friend's mother about the night before her brother died. She claimed to be awakened in the middle of the night by an angel standing at the foot of her bed. The angel said nothing. She stretched out her hand toward my friend's startled aunt. In her hand, she held her brother's ring. The angel closed the ring in her fist, and then she was gone. The woman specifically said the angel was a woman. Yet, in the Bible, angels are usually depicted as men. By morning, my friend's aunt got word of her brother's death.

I remember thinking, do angels make such appearances? Do angels warn us of upcoming events such as deaths? Was the elderly woman really awake, or was this vision in a dream? That said, the accuracy of the vision, dream, or physical experience was incredibly spot on. The woman seemed comforted by the angel's visit rather than frightened, and when the morning came and she received the terrible news, she felt blessed to have been warned by one of God's heavenly beings.

In hindsight, I wish I would've had the fortitude to ask questions, but I was young, a teenager. I was more spellbound by what I was hearing, though I remember having questions and I still do.

Perhaps angels do come in different forms, so we are not frightened by their appearance. Our God is a merciful God. He touches us with gentle comfort. He knows our heart. He knows how to communicate with us...even if it's through an angel we can identify as an angel, like the one who visited my friend's aunt, or a stranger who assists us with a flat tire. After all Hebrews 13:2 tells us, *Do not neglect to show hospitality to strangers, for thereby some have entertained angels, unawares.*

PRAYER

Dearest, merciful Lord, bless us with your gentle, compassionate touch, and help us to be gentle and compassionate toward others, always.

Amen.

DECEMBER 7TH

MICHAH 5:2

But you, Bethlehem Ephrathah, though you are small among the clans of Judah, out of you will come for me one who will be ruler over Israel, whose origins are from of old, from ancient times.

I live in a small, obscure, rural town with a funny name. Every August the town has a rather large fair. Other than that, nothing particularly exciting or newsworthy comes from my town. I don't know about the town you live in, big or small, but when the teens from our area reach their senior year of high school, they exclaim, *I can't wait to graduate! I can't wait to get out of this podunk place!* And in the fall, they leave for faraway universities with anticipations of something far grander than the trivial little town with the funny name. It isn't long until they discover home wasn't so bad after all. Now, not all of them return, but I must say a good portion of them do. Small towns are great places to raise children.

One has to wonder if the youth who were growing up in Bethlehem at the time of Jesus's birth felt the same. From all accounts, Bethlehem was a fairly insignificant little village. But oh, what an unexpected, wonderful event would transpire in this irrelevant place! In fact, in Hebrew, the name "Bethlehem" translates to "house of bread." And as Jesus proclaimed, "*I am the bread of life*" (John 6:35;48).

Can you even begin to imagine? You are a young teen in Bethlehem, and when you come of age, possibly marry, your only intention is to move away from this dull, extraneous location. Perhaps Jerusalem or Nazareth would be more exciting.

And then…

A baby is born in a lowly cave/stable at the very edge of Bethlehem, and he would be the savior of the world. Jesus was not the expected Messiah. The jews of his day were not looking for a tiny baby wrapped in swaddling clothes. No. They were anticipating a great warrior. They were in search of a soldier to fight immense battles on their behalf. Instead, they or we received a Savior. We received the bread of life, a good shepherd who healed the sick, fed five-thousand, raised Lazarus from the dead, and suffered and died on the cross to save *everyone* from sin.

So, what are you anticipating in this season of Advent? What will you do with the greatest gift of all—the good shepherd, the bread of life, the Savior, Jesus Christ?

PRAYER

Lord in heaven, let us be thankful this season of
Advent, and well afterward.

Let us be most thankful for the greatest gift of all, the
good shepherd, the bread of life, Jesus Christ.

Amen.

DECEMBER 8TH

JOHN 15:16

YOU DID NOT CHOOSE ME, BUT I CHOSE YOU. AND I AP-
POINTED YOU TO GO AND BEAR FRUIT, FRUIT THAT WILL
LAST, SO THAT THE FATHER WILL GIVE YOU WHATEVER
YOU ASK HIM IN MY NAME.

"CHOOSE YOUR FRIENDS WISELY," my mother used to say,
and yes, I've repeated that advice to my girls on many an
occasion. As we travel through life, friends are important.
They are an integral part of who we become. Over the
years and the decades, our friends change as we change
or our adult life takes us to different places, both physical and emotional. It is so important to have good friends;
those who we can depend on in times of turmoil, someone to share a secret with, knowing the secret is safe.

Oftentimes we're seeking advice from our friend, or we simply need to talk when we're feeling frustrated with life. A good friend is always there to offer support when needed.

In today's busy world, it seems most people don't have lifelong friendships. I am blessed to have several girlfriends who I have been friends with for…well, almost forever. When I have lunch with any one of my friends, we discuss all things. As the years have paraded by, our conversations have turned to our faith and how it has changed and grown since our youth.

"You did not choose me, but I chose you," Jesus explains to his disciples. That's right. Jesus chooses us, and make no mistake, we too are his disciples. Jesus does not make distinctions based on our merits. We are not, because we surely *cannot* be chosen by our qualifications. Jesus wants you, me, and *everyone* to be his friend. A friend who can be called upon in times of distress, joy, heartbreak, and advice. Jesus is an excellent secret-keeper, too.

"I appointed you to bear fruit, fruit that will last…" Jesus expounds his message to his disciples to spread the gospel and to be an example for all people. Likewise, he is asking us to do the same. Most of us, including myself, are shy about spreading the good news and that's okay. There are many ways to lead, and they don't require standing up

in front of large crowds.

Many years ago, my father was having a heart procedure. My mother and I were sitting in a surgical waiting room. A surgeon came into the room and directed a woman who was sitting alone to follow him into the nearby conference room. The conference room had large windows, and we could see them talking. It was clear the surgeon was not giving the woman good news, and when they emerged from the room, he was patting her back as she wept. He instructed her to have a seat, and someone would come for her. Mom and I exchanged worried glances as the woman sat down, buried her face in a tissue, and sobbed. Mom didn't hesitate. She got right up, went to the coffee service, poured a cup, and took it to the woman. Mom sat down next to her, wrapped her arm around her, and the woman laid her head on Mom's shoulder to cry. At that very moment, Mom was bearing the fruit Jesus was speaking of, and yes, it was fruit that would last. I will never forget that moment, and I have no doubt the woman did either.

Lastly, Jesus told the disciples, *"...so that the Father will give you whatever you ask him in my name."* Indeed. The power of prayer is very real. I've seen first-hand the strength of prayers for someone in cancer treatment, and the peace prayer brings to those who are mourning.

When we speak to our Father in Jesus's glorious name, *all things* are possible.

Choose your friends wisely—this was and always will be excellent advice. Choosing Jesus, walking with Jesus, and, of course, talking with Jesus is the best advice ever given.

PRAYER

Dearest Father, help us to always choose Jesus.
Encourage us to bear the fruit of your word, and
always call upon you for our needs.
Indeed, we have a true and faithful friend in our
Savior, Jesus.
Bring us to him in times of joy, sorrow, victory, and
defeat.
In Jesus's victorious name.

Amen.

DECEMBER 9TH

JOHN 10:11

I AM THE GOOD SHEPHERD: THE GOOD SHEPHERD GIVES
HIS LIFE FOR THE SHEEP.

NOT FAR FROM MY HOUSE, there is a sheep farm. I pass
the farm often; after all, it sits right along the main highway. In the winter, the flock is wooly, giving passersby
the impression they are very large, fat sheep. And then
in the springtime, the farmer has the flock sheered. Sud-
denly, they look much smaller, skinnier. I find it interesting that I never see the farmer, the shepherd of the
flock. I never see him walking through the field, tossing
hay bales for the sheep to nibble on, and yet, in the winter months, the hay is there for the flock. They seem per-
fectly comfortable to be in the pasture, grazing, caring for

themselves, and not particularly worried about predators. Still…where is the farmer, the good shepherd? Is the farmer a man or a woman? I haven't a clue. However, I'm sure the sheep know them, especially at feeding time.

David said to Saul, *"Your servant used to be a shepherd for his father. And when there came a lion or a bear and took a lamb from the flock, I went after it and struck him and delivered the lamb from his mouth. And if he rose against me, I caught him by his beard, and struck him, and killed him"* (1 Samuel 17: 34-35). Quite frankly, in my little corner of Pennsylvania, I doubt the local sheep farmer worries too much about a lion or a bear attacking his flock like David. Still, no one appears to be tending the sheep.

Recently, as the day was giving way to dusk, I drove past the sheep farm, and the sheep weren't grazing quietly. Instead, they were bunched tightly together and running in a circle. It looked quite chaotic. I slowed down to see what might be wrong, but I couldn't discern the problem. There was no big dog or coyote chasing them, so what was the matter?

As I continued on my way, I couldn't shake the image of the sheep running in the panicked circle. Yet nothing was there to cause such panic, nor was the farmer there to protect them. I couldn't help but contemplate the sheep, and as I did, a parallel thought crossed my mind. The flock's fright is much like our life. We find ourselves running in circles after or away from an invisible force that frightens us, threatens us, bullies us, and yet we can't put our finger on what it is. We watch the news, scroll through social media, and read the newspaper. Trouble seems to be everywhere, even in places we'd always deemed as safe-havens: school, church, the supermarket. So often, the world seems to be in a wicked wreck. What is going on? How do we cope? Who do we turn to?

We are very similar to the sheep in the field scrambling from something we cannot find, foresee, or control. Oftentimes, that something is masked.

So, where is *our* shepherd?

Where do we find this dependable, faithful shepherd?

Jesus said, "*I am the good shepherd: who gives his life for the sheep.*" In this verse, Jesus identifies himself as a leader, a caretaker who is willing to put his life down for his flock, and of course, to fulfill the scriptures, Jesus died on the cross. Clearly, in John 10:11, Jesus is not speaking of the wooly sheep in the field, but rather of God's people, us. He is reaching out to us, trying to connect, wanting to soothe our worried minds, and walk with us through all of our distress.

But do we know this shepherd?

Do we *try* to know him, or does he get lost in the shuffle of our everyday chaos?

It is easy to stare at our problems and not know where to turn.

If this Advent season finds you feeling lost, abandoned, or overwhelmed, please know Jesus is waiting. He is waiting for you to call upon him. He is just a whispered prayer away. Jesus is anticipating the moment he becomes *your* good shepherd.

PRAYER

Dearest Lord in heaven, thank you for sending our good shepherd, Jesus.

Please help us turn to Jesus in times of sorrow or distress.

Help us to call upon him always, and ask him to be our good shepherd, our good and faithful friend.

Amen.

DECEMBER 10TH

MATTHEW 6:34

So, do not worry about tomorrow, for tomorrow will bring worries of its own. Today's trouble is enough for today.

ANXIETY—WE SEE IT EVERYWHERE and perhaps experience it ourselves. Today's verse beckons us to live in the present and trust in God to provide what we need and to resolve whatever conflict is causing us despair. As humans, it is hard, if not almost impossible, to let go of our need to be in complete control, and there lies much of our angst.

I must admit, I can be a bit of a control freak. I'm an *everything has a place and everything in its place* kind of person. And yes, that has caused a bit of...fuss in our home from time-to-time.

While my husband, Bill, and I were on vacation in Michigan, we were driving along a dark, winding highway. We hit a very large raccoon. The raccoon broke apart the lower half of our grill and pretty much everything attached. Long story short, we drove all the way back to Pennsylvania with zip-ties holding the front our vehicle together. The day the appraiser was supposed to come to our house to evaluate the damage; I had an appointment. In other words, I needed my vehicle. Trouble was, the appraiser was supposed to call the morning of my appointment, and yes, I was fretting. Did I mention I'm a very scheduled person, too? This also can be the crux of anxiety.

Bill said, "No problem. You'll just have to take the pickup truck."

No problem? I considered this a *big* problem. I felt the apprehension welling up inside of me. I'm not accustomed to driving the pickup. It's big, and in *my* mind, intimidating. I didn't want to drive the truck fifteen miles and down some pretty long, steep hills into town for my appointment. I was hoping when the appraiser called to make the appointment, he'd set the time for long after I had returned home so I could take my vehicle. Indeed, I was allowing the troubles of tomorrow to wreck today. Bill was rolling his eyes.

So, was the appraiser's appointment convenient to my time dilemma?

No such luck.

"You'll be okay," Bill assured me when he got off the phone. "You used to drive our trucks all the time." His voice had an edge of frustration left over from yesterday's fussing. Regardless, I soon found myself climbing into the pickup and driving along our back roads toward town.

I kept reprimanding myself. "He's right. What's wrong with me? Why am I so afraid of this silly pickup truck?" And yet, the anxiety wouldn't release its grip. Well, I made it to my appointment with no mishaps along the way, and yet when I approached the truck in the parking lot to go home, there it was again—the fear of driving that monster home.

I climbed back into the truck, closed my eyes, took several deep breaths, and did what I should have done yesterday: I talked with God. I told him that I knew he was sitting next to me, and he would drive all the way home with me, as he had traveled to town with me. I thanked him for delivering me to my appointment safely, and when I opened my eyes, guess what? The stress had melted away.

God was there for me.

The fact is, God is *always* there for me. He is always

there for all of us. He is no more than a prayer away. He takes care of our todays, and he is present in all of our tomorrows, well before the morning even dawns. *He is there. He is always there.*

Prayer

Mighty Lord, help us.

Help us leave the worries of tomorrow with you, knowing you are always there before tomorrow dawns.

Encourage us to allow you to place your comforting hand on our shoulder to soothe the worries of today.

Travel with us, oh, Lord.

In Jesus's blessed name.

Amen.

A Gentle Reflection

The roads we trek are sometimes long, dark,
and winding.

When the wind blows and rustles the trees,
we feel lost and afraid.

When the rain pelts our face, we feel defeated.
Who can we turn to when rejection stings
our ears?

We have a strong hand to cling to.
We have a willing ear to speak into.

There is never an inconvenient moment to
talk or to explain.

It is always the right time to speak and know
you will be heard.

You will be seen.
You are important.
You are loved.

For *you* are *His* child.

C.S. McDonald

DECEMBER 11TH

LUKE 9:23-24

AND JESUS SAID TO ALL, "IF ANYONE WOULD COME AFTER ME, LET HIM DENY HIMSELF AND TAKE UP HIS CROSS DAILY AND FOLLOW ME. FOR WHOEVER WOULD SAVE HIS LIFE WILL LOSE IT, BUT WHOEVER LOSES HIS LIFE FOR MY SAKE WILL SAVE IT."

WOW. THAT'S ONE SCARY BIBLE VERSE. Fear not. Jesus isn't asking us to die on a cross as he did, and in turn, securing our place in eternity. Rather, he is urging us to follow him in order to ensure eternity for ourselves. *For God so loved the world, that he gave his only begotten Son, that whoever believes in him should not perish but have everlasting life* (John 3:16).

Jesus's statement is actually broken down in one simple request: *follow me*. Jesus's short ministry was a model of how we can live our lives, even in today's world. Life is complicated. The rules we live by can become hazy at times, and the path Jesus asks us to trod can be difficult, especially by today's standards. Let me assure you, the path Jesus walked was more than difficult. The politics and social impact were as complex as they are today, and not in very different ways. He loved the unlovable, fed the hungry, and healed the sick and lame. Meanwhile, Jesus was well aware of the outcome: laying down his life for ours.

So, how do we follow Jesus? The journey in faith is different for each of us. Jesus isn't asking for faultlessness. Instead, he offers us one clear-cut invitation: *follow me*. Yes, he wants you to follow him in your daily life. He asks *you* to be an example wherever you go, and to allow him into your decisions through prayer. He has sent the Holy Spirit to help guide your way. If you are uncertain, ask Jesus, how shall I follow you? How can *I* be an example? Sit quietly. Listen. He will show you the way.

PRAYER

Dear God, please help me follow Jesus.

Help me be the example you want me to be.

Help me, in this busy world to take time, be still and
listen.

Let Jesus take my hand and lead me along the path
you wish me to follow.

Amen.

DECEMBER 12TH

PSALM 139:1-2

YOU HAVE SEARCHED ME LORD, AND YOU KNOW ME. YOU KNOW WHEN I SIT DOWN AND WHEN I STAND UP; YOU DISCERN MY THOUGHTS FROM FAR AWAY.

GOD IS NEVER FAR AWAY. I can feel his presence in my daily errands and tasks. I know he is with me in my going out and my coming in. He knows my worries, my likes and dislikes. Regrettably, he is aware of my addiction to chocolate. And yes, he knows my most inner thoughts, good and bad.

We cannot hide from God. He is our Father, our maker, and he knows us more intimately than we know ourselves, or than we are willing to know ourselves. He knows what is in our heart and our soul.

Sometimes we do or say things we don't mean. And every so often we say things we should keep to ourselves but fail miserably and let them tumble out with disastrous results.

I am painfully guilty of these transgressions.

The fact is, we *all* are. Oftentimes, it is hard to admit to ourselves that we are guilty of hurting or offending another person with words or actions. We don't like to believe, or perhaps confess, we are capable of doing such things, yet it happens. And when it does, what should we do? How do we make it right with the individual and with God?

Firstly, we have to calm down. After a squabble, emotions can run fast and loose. Taking time to settle ourselves and honestly consider what took place can be truly freeing. Certainly, an apology may be in order, but first, talk with him who knows your feelings and your thoughts. Talk with God. The truth is never hidden from God. He knows. He understands, and he loves us unconditionally. We are blessed with his grace.

Today's verse is a clear reminder of God's boundless presence and his complete understanding of the human soul. It also suggests a call to self-reflection; to know and have a deeper relationship with God.

Advent is a good time to find a quiet place and

reflect on our difficult moments. God is anticipating your prayer. He is waiting for you to talk to him about those transgressions you've been holding inside, whatever they may be. God is waiting and his grace is never-ending.

PRAYER

Dearest Lord in heaven, help me find a way to let go
of the transgressions I've been holding deep inside.
You know my heart.
Help me find the courage to speak freely and release
my burden into your boundless grace.

Amen.

DECEMBER 13TH

ACTS 20:35

IN ALL ACTS THAT I HAVE SHOWN YOU THAT BY WORKING HARD IN THIS WAY WE MUST HELP THE WEAK AND REMEMBER THE WORDS OF LORD JESUS, HOW HE HIMSELF SAID, "IT IS MORE BLESSED TO GIVE THAN TO RECEIVE."

MOST OF MY FRIENDS WILL TELL YOU that I am a talker. I have a dear friend who has traveled for years with me to books signings and, God bless her, used to man the backstage area for my dance recitals. Let me tell you, getting little girls and even teenagers to the stage on time and keeping them quiet requires nothing less than divine intervention. Anyway, Linda likes to tell everyone that I have the gift of gab. She claims that I can talk to anyone, anywhere, and at any time. I suppose she's not exaggerating.

I do like to talk and meet people. Over the years, I've met many interesting people with interesting stories. However, I'm also someone who likes to smile. While walking through our local mall, I smile at complete strangers all the time. Most of the time, they return my smile, and they appear genuinely happy to have received a smile.

My mother used to work as the secretary for the principal at a large high school in our area. She used to tell me, "*Cindy, it's best to be kind to people. You just don't know what they've been through before they left the house in the morning.*" I took Mom's statement to heart, and I smile when I come upon everyone I meet. Hey, it may be the only smile they receive that day.

One day I went into the bank, and the teller seemed to be in a foul mood. She wasn't very cordial to the person before me in line. When I stepped up to the window, I could see at some point she'd been crying. I passed my banking across the desk to her and noticed she was wearing a brooch. "That's a beautiful brooch you're wearing. I just love brooches," I told her.

Immediately, her hand caressed the brooch. "This was my mother's. She passed away last month, and I miss her so much," she said.

I reached across the desk to place my hand gently on

hers. "Losing a mom is the hardest of heartaches," I said.

She dragged her gaze to meet mine and favored me with a watery smile.

When Jesus said, "*It is more blessed to give than to receive.*" He was speaking of our time, talents, and, yes, our compassion for others. Sharing something as simple as a smile can mean so much to the person on the receiving end. Sometimes someone who seems to be out of sorts might actually be hurting. It is best to be gentle with them rather than match their ill temper with more.

It is the season of Advent. The season of anticipating. The season of giving and if you're giving away a smile, go ahead, add a *Merry Christmas*. I do and more times than not, I get one back.

PRAYER

Gracious Father, in this season of Advent, and every season, help us find a way to give of ourselves, even in the simplest of ways.

Help us to be an example of your compassionate grace.

Amen.

December 14th

Colossians 2:9-10

For in him the whole fullness of deity dwells bodily, in Christ you have been brought to fullness. He is the head over every ruler and authority.

The call for perfection seems to come at us from every direction. As age creeps into our reality, we often succumb to those calls. We find ourselves dipping into the fountain of youth with creams, masks, facial treatments, while some resort to surgeries, and as we've seen on social media, many of those surgeries have proven disastrous. And then there's the gym. You can't see me, of course, but as I wrote that last short sentence, I was wincing. We dub all of these rituals as *aging gracefully*.

We hold ourselves to high standards that seemingly

measure our worth: what social circle we travel in, where we work, how much money we make, what kind of vehicle we drive, and of course, our appearance is at the pinnacle of our self-worth. These mindsets can easily become the ruler and authority over our lives.

Likewise, celebrities are held in the highest esteem. They are the embodiment of perfection in so many people's eyes. The flawless body, impeccable fashion, perfect life, and yet they don't know us, and we certainly don't know them. Do the people we admire, celebrity or not, have what we *think* they have? Are they happier than we are because of what they have, or do we *perceive* them as happy? Are they truly complete in their picture-perfect lifestyles? One might wonder: who is *their* ruler and authority?

When I was a professional dancer and choreographer, I owned a small dance school in my small town. I used to admire the large *successful* dance schools in the surrounding towns who serviced as many as three-hundred-plus students. They made so much money. They all drove BMWs, Cadillacs, and sports cars. On the surface, they seemed to have it all, and for many years, I envied them. As time rolled by, I came to realize that it wasn't them who were so lucky and I wasn't *lucky* either. I was *blessed.* God had blessed me with a small, successful school in a rural town. I also owned the tiny building that housed my school. For me, dance season ran from Labor Day through April. The bigger schools housed in large, rented spaces had to run through June. My school was closed on Saturdays. The other dance owners were open on Saturdays to accommodate the number of students they had. I didn't run summer dance camps. Instead, I attended my daughters' horse shows and family gatherings. No, I didn't make as much money as they did, but God put me in a place where kids *needed* a dance school, and blessed me with family time, and the joy of freedom all summer long. I was also blessed with a wonderful, supportive husband.

When I retired from my dance career in 2011, and started my writing career, I didn't obsess over becoming a best-selling author. I knew God would direct me where I needed to be, where he wanted me to be, and I've done okay. Am I on the same lists as James Patterson? Not hardly. And I'm okay with that because I know God is in control, and I feel complete in that knowledge.

Giving the reins to God and having a solid relationship with Christ frees us from the demands of human authorities. Aging in grace is way better than aging gracefully. God does not expect perfection. Not from us. Not ever. God has blessed us with his son to be our Savior and he is the true head of every ruler and authority. God wants us to unite with him and find completeness in Jesus.

PRAYER

Loving Lord, perfection is an impossible goal.
Let me walk in the confidence of knowing Jesus,
finding joy in his presence, and abandoning all envy
in those who I think have a better life than mine.
Help me age with grace, leaving behind the rulers
and authorities of humanity, and always find completeness in your son, Jesus.

Amen.

December 15th

Isaiah 40:31

But they who wait for the Lord shall renew their strength; they shall mount up with wings like eagles; they shall run and not be weary; they shall walk and not faint.

Waiting is such a hard thing to do, especially in this age of instant gratification. Everything is a mere click away, always within our reach. We are no longer accustomed to waiting. Yet in today's verse, we are promised a renewal of strength in waiting. We will soar like eagles without limitations when we are confident in the Lord. We can run and not grow weary and walk without fainting when our full and unwavering trust is placed in his powerful, loving hands.

Turning to God during frightening times or when we feel disheartened can fill us with courage and hope. Our verse today reminds us to seek God's strength when we feel crushed by life's disappointments or difficult circumstances.

In 2010, my mother was diagnosed with Alzheimer's disease. How could this be? This woman was the strongest person I knew. Resolute. Determined. Organized to a fault, and she was not to be challenged when I was growing up. My mother was four-foot-eleven inches of tough stuff.

By 2012, Mom could no longer stay in her home. I tried to have her live with me. No way. She would march into my living room every morning with suitcase in hand, and insist, "I'm going home *now*, Cynthia." And no matter how I tried to reason with her, it was her way or the highway.

My brother lived right next door from my mom. We decided to try visiting nurses. She'd throw them out of the house. My brother would find her wandering around the yard looking for my father. Like me, my brother lives rurally, and he was terrified she'd wander off, and something awful would happen to her in the woods. My older brother said, "I know you want Mom to get better, but it just isn't going to happen. It's time, Cindy.

For her own safety, and our peace of mind, we need to put her in a facility."

I thought the day my father died was the worst day of my life. I was wrong. The worst day of my life was when my brother and I delivered Mom to the assisted living facility. The facility was beautiful, and the staff was wonderful. Nevertheless, to say she was upset would be the understatement of the century. Mom was straight up hopping mad.

And so the ten-year struggle with Alzheimer's disease truly began. Mom was combative. When I would visit, she would scream and yell at me. After weeks of horrible visits, I was told by the head nurse that I could not visit without my brother. I was what they called a "*trigger.*" When I showed up, all the distress of the disease walked through the door with me. She wanted to go home. She wanted to know where Dad was. She wanted to talk with her father.

I was at wits' end.

I would toss in my bed at night with anxiety attacks. Had I done the wrong thing? What else could I do? I was at the point where I hated my bed. I was like a child who hated nighttime and didn't want to go to bed. I was exhausted. Emotionally drained. I needed help, but I truly didn't know where to turn. Was God my first go-to? No.

The anxiety attacks worsened. Finally, they medicated Mom, and things calmed down quite a bit. Still, I didn't turn to God, and yet, as I look back, he was there. He was walking alongside me all the way.

God was waiting for me.

Oftentimes, God shows us the way in everyday things. One afternoon, I was scrolling through social media, and I came upon a meditation guru. Cautiously enticed, I tapped the link and listened. Then I took my laptop back to my bed and participated in the breathing exercises, and the meditative mantras the soft-spoken man was demonstrating. God was speaking to me through the man. He was saying, it's all in hand. Trust me. I am here. I am *always* here. I continued the meditation exercises for several weeks. Things continued to improve, and I was able to face my bed and sleep. I calmed down and finally started talking with God, and he helped to ease my troubled mind.

As the years marched by, Mom no longer recognized us, but we visited anyway. She was our mom, and we loved her. When our visits were over my brother would kiss her and tell her he loved her, and I would do the same, and sometimes we would receive a gift, and absolute blessing...Mom would manage to mutter, "I love you, too." By 2019, mom was blind and spoke very little. When she spoke, it was more of a mumble, undecipherable. At this point, she'd been wheelchair bound for about three years.

They say those who have been ill with cancer or a disease such as Alzheimer's seemed to be sitting in God's waiting room. Waiting for his call to come home. For my brother and I, that statement rang very true. She waited. We waited. Yes, we were waiting on God, and I turned to him, only this time, asking for him to take her. It was time to take her home.

We lost mom in October 2020. The long, dark road of Alzheimer's disease prepared me for Mom's death, and it taught me to turn to God first. Since then, I trust the Lord to handle my every worry, and anxiety does not come knocking at my bedroom door at night. If I'm feeling bothered by something, I give it to God. I soar like that eagle into the clouds and sleep, confident that all is in hand, because he is there through the night and well into tomorrow.

It's true. In this twenty-first century life of ours, we wait for nothing. We depend on the physical *things* that bring us instant results. Are we willing to wait for God? The real reality is, God is always willing to wait for us because he loves us— all of us.

Trust in the Lord. You shall run and not be weary. You shall walk and not faint.

PRAYER

Dearest Lord, your grace is so beautiful.

It is endless.

Help me always trust in you; to call out to you first
before moving forward.

Waiting is so difficult.

Help me soar like an eagle into your loving
compassion.

Amen.

A Gentle Reflection

There's a whisper on a breeze cajoling me
to listen, yet I continue on my way without
hesitation.

My boots crunch the fallen leaves, persuading
me to pause and clear my tangled thoughts
with your subtle call.

Yet still, I walk the path, not aware you simply
want to talk.

You are waiting.
I am preoccupied.
But with what?
What can I keep from you?
You know my thoughts, my worries, my sins.
Your grace is boundless.

I stop and look around at the almost barren
trees and the clouds slowly
wafting in the afternoon sky.

There is no other more perfect place to talk
with you than here amongst your creation.
I bow my head and pour my heart.

C.S. McDonald

DECEMBER 16TH

JOHN 8:12

I AM THE LIGHT OF THE WORLD. WHOEVER FOLLOWS ME, WILL NEVER WALK IN DARKNESS, BUT WILL HAVE THE LIGHT OF LIFE.

WHAT A POWERFUL STATEMENT Jesus makes in today's verse. It is more than just a declaration; it is our true, un-wavering salvation. As we have all experienced, the sea-sons don't always flow unerringly past. Each season can bring its own fury. And with nature's angry winds or heavy snowfalls comes the unpleasantness of power outages. Recently, one such wicked storm trampled my tri-state area, and the outages ran far and wide for well over a week. Many were walking in darkness, anxiously waiting for the electricity to come back on, and oh, what a relief when the house was filled with light once again.

Truly, our daily life can be much like a power outage, walking in the darkness of uncertainty or sorrow. Jesus's light pierces the barriers of *all* darkness to lead us out of all insecurities and grief.

Whoever follows me, will never walk in darkness, but will have the light of life. No. Jesus is not promising our lives will be perfect, without dilemma, sorrow, or loss. Rather, he offers his hand to guide us through those moments. The light of Christ is a beacon through the darkness, so we no longer wander aimlessly in the shadows without answers. He is the *light of life*, our spiritual guide, and the *only* path to God's everlasting truth, grace, and eternal life.

Jesus wants us to *follow him*, urging us to make a commitment, live our lives by his example, and place our trust in him. This Advent season, renew your trust in Jesus and let him guide you along whatever path you are walking.

PRAYER

Dearest Jesus, please be my light; the beacon in my
darkness.
Let me walk confidently through this broken world
and carry your light with me.
Help me live by your example and help others pierce
the darkness, too.
In your holy, beautiful name.

Amen.

December 17th

Luke 2:8-11

In that region there were shepherds living in the fields, keeping watch over their flocks by night. Then an angel of the Lord stood before them, and the glory of the Lord shone around them, and they were terrified. But the angel said to them, "Do not be afraid, for see—I am bringing you good news of great joy for all the people: To you is born this day in the city of David a Savior, who is the Messiah."

I love the shepherds. I especially love the children who represent the shepherds in our church's annual Christmas program. They look so cute in their bathrobes, a towel of some sort wrapped around their heads, and a pair of flip-flops on their feet. It's never out of the question for a sword fight to break out during a rehearsal with the shepherd's staffs repurposed as a sword or a lightsaber. Sound effects included, of course.

Cajoling kids to learn lines is usually an exercise in futility. Even if they do learn them, there comes that moment in the program when someone inevitably forgets the next line. Everyone freezes, and they exchange wide-eyed glances at each other that silently scream, *Whose line is it?* There's always that one kid who's rolling their eyes because they know whose line it is. Sometimes their frustration will get the best of them, and they'll blurt it out for the absent-minded child.

Actually, I think this little scene playing out before us with assumed dialogue between the shepherds on the hill near Bethlehem isn't too far off point. While Luke doesn't give us an account of their conversation until the angel has left them, and to be honest, some time to calm down, I believe the wide-eyed reaction would be spot-on. Although, I also believe there would've been some screaming, perhaps several ran away to watch from a distance, and those who were brave enough to hold their ground, or too terrified to move, were most likely shaking in their sandals.

After all, why would an angel of the Lord come

to tell *them*? The shepherds. This group of people was considered some of the lowest form of humans. They were not a respected bunch. And yet, an *angel* came to tell *them* of Jesus's birth. Some of the lowliest members of society knew before anyone else of the Messiah's arrival. God does not hold up the wealthy or socialites above all others. He loves us all, includes us all, even the lowly shepherds on a hill near Bethlehem. And the shepherds responded. They traveled to Bethlehem to see this baby the angel told them about. They wanted to meet the Messiah. Who, as it turns out, was to be the Good Shepherd.

PRAYER

Thank you, Lord, for sending Jesus to us and loving us so much you would send your only begotten son to draw us closer to you.

Help us to walk joyfully during these final days of Advent and every day in the anticipation of Lord Jesus's return.

Amen.

December 18th

Romans 15:13

May the God of hope fill you with all joy and peace in believing, so by the power of the Holy Spirit you may abound in hope.

Our God truly is the God of hope. We are seven days away from Christmas, and I hope this verse finds you in good spirits and filled with optimism for today and the future. God is the fountain and giver of hope. As believers, we are truly aware of this fact. However, the holidays can be a stressful time, especially as we draw closer to the big day. There is so much to be done; shopping, baking, gift wrapping, parties to attend, family gatherings, and yes, those family get-togethers can be the source of some stress. God has given us great resources to battle all of our holiday anxiety, if we simply employ them.

Our verse tells us God will fill us with *all joy and peace in believing.* Essentially, peace and joy, not just during the holidays, but every day, come from trusting in God. Our peace is not derived from our own ability to create it, but in our ability to stop, take a breath, and then talk with God before stepping into that family gathering, or the Christmas party where we come face-to-face with tricky relationships or people we simply don't like.

Of course, intricate gatherings are not exclusive to the holidays. Life events such as our children's weddings can steal away all joy and peace when we must come together with a former spouse or mother-in-law. Certainly, avoiding our former spouse during the wedding is usually the cure, yet the shiver of awkwardness eventually erupts at some point: photo sessions or during those special parent/child dances. God doesn't want your peace to be destroyed during any special event, the holidays or otherwise. He wants to fill you with joy and peace within your believing and trust in him. Keeping God close, through prayer and reflection, when we find ourselves in these uncomfortable circumstances is the true cure for our insecurities.

Our verse also reminds us that we are always surrounded by the Holy Spirit, whose power helps us to achieve God's abounding hope. He has provided resources to assist us, but it is up to us to utilize them in order to experience His joy and peace, always.

PRAYER

Thank you, God for loving us and always being within our reach to help us through a difficult time. You are a loving father who brings us hope and joy and peace by the power of the Holy Spirit.

Help us to talk to you when we feel our confidence waning, allow the Holy Spirit to help us renew our trust and faith always.

In Jesus's holy name.

Amen.

DECEMBER 19TH

MARY'S SONG OF PRAISE

LUKE 1:46-56

46 AND MARY SAID, "MY SOUL MAGNIFIES THE LORD,

47 AND MY SPIRIT REJOICES IN GOD MY SAVIOR,

48 FOR HE HAS LOOKED WITH FAVOR ON THE LOWLINESS OF HIS SERVANT. SURELY, FROM NOW ON ALL GENERATIONS WILL CALL ME BLESSED;

49 FOR THE MIGHTY ONE HAS DONE GREAT THINGS FOR ME, AND HOLY IS HIS NAME.

50 HIS MERCY IS FOR THOSE WHO FEAR HIM FROM GENERATION TO GENERATION.

51 HE HAS SHOWN STRENGTH WITH HIS ARM; HE HAS SCATTERED THE PROUD IN THE THOUGHTS OF THEIR HEARTS.

52 HE HAS BROUGHT DOWN THE POWERFUL FROM

THEIR THRONES, AND LIFTED UP THE LOWLY.

53 HE HAS FILLED THE HUNGRY WITH GOOD THINGS AND SENT THE RICH AWAY EMPTY.

54 HE HAS HELPED HIS SERVANT ISREAL, IN THE REMEMBRANCE OF HIS MERCY,

55 ACCORDING TO THE PROMISE HE MADE TO OUR ANCESTORS, TO ABRAHAM AND TO HIS DESCENDANTS FOREVER."

56 AND MARY REMAINED WITH HER [ELIZABETH] ABOUT THREE MONTHS AND THEN RETURNED TO HER HOME.

MARY'S SONG OF PRAISE. Oh, how this song/poem touches my heart so deeply every time our congregation sings it during Lenten vespers. Remember, this beautiful praise to God was written by a *thirteen-year-old girl* who was recently visited by an angel and conceived God's child. I am truly awestruck when I think about the moment the angel appeared. Those circumstances would be scary for any woman, but for such a young girl, it had to be terrifying. After all, Mary was not married, only engaged, and yet Mary placed her trust in God. Such unmovable faith for a young girl.

Verses 48 and 49 are stunning: 48 *for he has looked with favor on the lowliness of his servant. Surely, from now on, all generations will call me blessed;* 49 *for the Mighty*

One has done great things for me, and holy is his name.

Mary declares her complete trust in God and knows the child she carries will change the world forever. She recognizes that God has chosen an everyday person to give birth to his son, and she feels blessed to be chosen.

How incredible is that?

No matter what your station if life, God sees you. God knows you. You are not invisible. You are God's child, and he loves you. Like Mary, the Mighty One has done great things for us by sending his only son to be our Savior.

Now, how incredible is *that*?

PRAYER

Mighty God, thank you for Mary.
Help us possess the faith and trust in you as Mary did.
Thank you for all the great things you have done for all of us. Thank you for Jesus.
Thank you for Advent.

Amen.

DECEMBER 20TH

MATTHEW 1:20-21

JOSEPH, SON OF DAVID, DO NOT BE AFRAID TO TAKE MARY AS YOU WIFE, FOR THE CHILD CONCEIVED IN HER IS FROM THE HOLY SPIRIT. SHE WILL BEAR A SON, AND YOU ARE TO NAME HIM, JESUS, FOR HE WILL SAVE HIS PEOPLE FROM THEIR SINS.

IMAGINE THE SHOCK FOR JOSEPH when he discovers his betrothed, Mary, is pregnant. I have no doubt he felt betrayed. Nevertheless, as he contemplates this new, unpleasant revelation, in his heart, he knows he cannot subject this young woman to public humiliation, possibly worse. I'm sure Joseph was hurting, and yet he was a good man. In Matthew verse 19, the Bible identifies him as a *righteous man*. Little did he know what would take place to change his life and the entire world, not just in the coming years, but forever.

God chose a common, but faithful, woman to bear his son. Likewise, he chose a common, but righteous, man to be his earthly dad. The Gospel of Matthew does not tell us when, how, nor the details of what Joseph planned to say to Mary, and most likely, Joseph was wondering the same. However, Joseph must've decided to sleep on it. Perhaps he had resolved to visit Mary the next day to discuss this devastating situation.

When I think about Joseph and his dilemma, I can imagine him lying down in his bed that night, staring at a ceiling, wondering how this could be. How could Mary deceive him this way? His heart had to have been heavy, and he surely wondered who she'd been with. The decision to dismiss her quietly was made, and after tossing in his bed, sleep finally overtook him. I imagine his sleep was deep when the angel appeared. In the scripture, Matthew does not tell us what the angel looked like, but this angel did not tell Joseph not to be afraid of him/her; rather, the angel told him not to be afraid to take Mary as his wife. The child she conceived was of the Holy Spirit, and the son she carried would save the people from their sins.

That's a lot to take in for a distraught man who, just hours ago, believed his betrothed had betrayed him.

Matthew tells us in verse 24, *When Joseph awoke from sleep, he did as the angel of the Lord commanded him; he took Mary as his wife.*

The Lord spoke to Joseph through an angel in a dream and when this man awoke, he felt reassured and blessed to be chosen by God to carry out and fulfill Isaiah's prophecy and God's promises. *Therefore, the Lord himself will give you a sign: the virgin will conceive and give birth to a son, and you will call him Immanuel* (Isaiah 7:14). His heart must've swelled in the knowledge that God chose him to care for his son, Immanuel. And so Joseph set all doubts aside, took up his faith, and he married Mary.

The faith and trust in God Joseph and Mary possessed was beyond our imagination. A thirteen-year-old girl's unwavering conviction to God and a man's fierce reliance in God's wisdom walked hand-in-hand, anticipating the delivery of the Messiah into a broken world. We are so very blessed for Mary and Joseph.

PRAYER

Dearest Lord, thank you for the faith and strength of Joseph and Mary.

Help me have the faith these two amazing people possessed.

Thank you for sending our Lord, Jesus Christ, for our salvation.

Amen.

A GENTLE REFLECTION

They'd run halfway down the staircase to peer
through the rail to see if the morning had
been delivered.

Are the gifts beneath the tree?

Has he come yet?

Then they'd come into my room to wake me.
"*Go get Mom and Dad*," they'd exclaim
in delight for the anticipating had
come to fruition.

I'd leap from my bed and scurry into Mom's
room. "*Come*," I'd squeal. "*He's been here!*"

Ah, Christmas morning memories.
The nativity sitting beneath the tree among
the glitter and flash of lights.

The true gift is there in the manger.

He's *been* here.
He's always *been* here.

Every Christmas morning, and every other
morning, God's gift, his son, our glorious
salvation, Jesus Christ.

C.S. McDonald

December 21st

Luke 2:3-4

All went to their own towns to be registered. Joseph also went from the town of Nazareth to Galilee to Judea, to the city of David called Bethlehem, because he was descended from the house and family of David.

When I look upon my nativity under the tree, my gaze seems to be drawn to the donkey munching hay in the background. I have two daughters and any woman who has given birth, especially naturally, wonders the same thing: how did Mary do it?

The Gospel of Luke doesn't reveal to us how much time has passed between the conception, Joseph's dream, and the summons to report to his hometown to be counted for the census. However, considering how quickly Mary gives birth when they finally arrive in Bethlehem, months must've gone by.

Now, while this is rather painful imagery, try to put yourself in Mary's place. You're very pregnant and riding on a *donkey*. The Bible does not tell us, but most likely Mary would have been seated on a pad or perhaps a blanket of some sort for *seventy* miles on a *donkey*. Provisions for the trip may have been in some kind of sack strapped to the donkey, so Mary's space would've been limited. It's very possible the journey to Bethlehem took place during the winter months. In that region, the temperature would have been in the thirties with potentially rainy conditions. On a *donkey*. The hilly trails would make traveling more challenging. I can imagine poor Mary clinging to the donkey's mane as she was bumped around.

To make matters worse, when they arrived in Bethlehem, all the rooms were taken. I'm sure we've all been in that position. A long trip to somewhere and when we arrive there's a concert or a big sporting event in town and all the hotel rooms are booked. Sorry, not quite the same. We may arrive at our destination tired and perhaps frustrated, but we traveled in the comfort of a motor vehicle.

This poor pregnant girl was no sooner informed her accommodations would be no better than the donkey she was riding upon that she went into labor and gave birth. I'm sure she was just as surprised as the rest of us that she was giving birth to the Messiah in a stable, or possibly a cave. But it was the way God wanted it to be. It was God's plan. Jesus was to be human. To experience his life as a human. Overcoming all the odds, feeling our pain and apprehensions, Jesus had to be like us in order for him to know compassion for God's people, and ultimately pay for our sins on the cross.

Jesus was given birth by a common, everyday woman who trudged along winding roads in the cold to give birth in an uncommon place. To give birth to the glorious Savior on our behalf.

Somehow, deep in my heart, I've got a feeling Mary gave that donkey a big hug when she was up to it. After all, that little donkey played an important and uncommon role in Jesus's birth and our salvation, as well.

PRAYER

Dear Lord, thank you for your faithfulness in keeping your promises.

Thank you for easy journeys and difficult ones too.

Thank you for always being with us during all of our
journeys.

Oh, and thank you for donkeys, too.

Amen.

DECEMBER 22ND

LUKE 2:6-7

WHILE THEY WERE THERE, THE TIME CAME FOR HER TO DELIVER HER CHILD. AND SHE GAVE BIRTH TO HER FIRST-BORN SON AND WRAPPED IN BANDS OF CLOTH, AND LAID HIM IN A MANGER, BECAUSE THERE WAS NO PLACE FOR THEM IN THE INN.

JESUS'S BIRTH IN SUCH AN UNLIKELY and lowly place emphasizes God's intention for his son's vulnerable and humble beginning. God wanted us to know that his love and grace is extended to everyone, including the poor and the marginalized. The choice of common people to carry out God's plan was just as intentional. Although Mary and Joseph were faithful servants, we do not earn God's love or favor through merit or good deeds.

We are accepted as we are, who we are, and wherever we are. God chooses *us* each and every time. Without reservation.

We are in the midst of anticipating the holidays. Meanwhile, God is *always* anticipating us. We are his sheep, and he has provided a Good Shepherd to gather us together under his umbrella of grace.

Mary wrapped her baby boy in bands of cloth and laid him in a manger. Were these the ideal conditions this young girl was anticipating? Absolutely not. Neither she nor Joseph was anticipating the trip to Bethlehem. Most likely, as any expectant mother, Mary was preparing a place for her newborn in their home. A clean, warm place to give birth and care for God's child. No doubt, that was *Mary's* plan. However, God had a different design and indeed, it would include a bit of hardship for his two faithful servants, but they answered the call, and they made the journey God intended his son to make. It was only just the beginning of the deliberate journey for Jesus, God's son, the Good Shepherd, our Savior.

PRAYER

Almighty God, I am awestruck by the birth of my
Savior, Jesus Christ.
I give you love and praise in the anticipation of our
Lord's coming.
Come, Lord Jesus.

Amen.

DECEMBER 23RD

JOHN 1:9

THE TRUE LIGHT, WHICH ENLIGHTENS EVERYONE, HAS COME INTO THE WORLD.

THE GOSPEL OF JOHN DECLARES JESUS as the *true* light. He is the foundation of spiritual enlightenment and leadership. John points out Jesus's light is offered to all people, no matter their sins or beliefs, gender, or culture. He gives light to everyone. Jesus's arrival, as announced earlier by John, "*the one who is coming after me; I am not worthy to untie the thong of his sandal*" (John 1:27). John goes on to testify in verse 34 that Jesus *is* "the son of God." Jesus's life and teachings will change the world forever, bringing love, compassion, and salvation for all people.

Look around. This is the season of Advent, and *everywhere* there is light. Lights strung on houses, twinkling on the Christmas trees, mantels decked with pine and illumination of tiny lights peek through the branches, and of course, the flicker of the Advent candles in the church. Christmas is the celebration of Jesus's birth, and we celebrate it with light. He is indeed the source of that light, and the truth that surpasses all understanding for all who seek him.

PRAYER

Thank you, dear Jesus for being the light of the world.
You are the light guiding us through this world, and
the light who leads us to the Father.
Please, Lord, always light our way.

Amen.

DECEMBER 24TH

ISAIAH 9:6

FOR A CHILD HAS BEEN BORN FOR US, A SON GIVEN TO
US; AUTHORITY RESTS UPON HIS SHOULDERS; AND HE IS
NAMED WONDERFUL COUNSELOR, MIGHTY GOD, EVER-
LASTING FATHER, PRINCE OF PEACE.

AND NOW MY FRIENDS, all the Advent candles have been
lit, and the church is glowing with all the anticipation of
Advent...

Hope gleams, anticipating the coming of the Messiah.

Peace glows brightly, remembering Mary and
Joseph's journey to Bethlehem and the peace Christ's birth
brings.

Shepherd flickers, anticipating the arrival of the
Savior.

Angel shimmers, filling us with the love and promise Christ's birth has brought into the world.

For a child is born, the Messiah came as a vulnerable little baby. *A son is given to us.* God's son brought into this world as a human being for the salvation of all peoples. And yes, *authority rests upon his shoulders*, for he will carry the burden of leading his people. And he is named, *Wonderful Counselor*, with wisdom and teachings the Messiah will tender. *Mighty God*, divinity with power and authority. *Everlasting Father*, an eternal loving father for his people, and *Prince of Peace*, reconnecting Almighty God in peace and grace with all humanity.

I love Christmas Eve. The love of God and our Savior, Jesus, swells in my heart. The candles cradled in the Advent wreath and those glimmering throughout the sanctuary in the congregation's hands as we softly sing *Silent Night* bring profound joy and inner peace. For now, the sweet baby sleeps in the manger, but oh, what wonderful things he will do, and we are saved because of one tiny, sleeping baby sent by God. Sleep gently, baby Jesus, for your work will begin soon, and oh, how all of humanity needed you then, and desperately need you now.

PRAYER

Dear God, you are an awesome God.
To love us so fully to send your son, Jesus, as our
Savior.
We are undeserving of your love, and yet with each
breath we take you love us more.
You know our heart.
Praise to you oh, God,
on this holy Christmas Eve.

Amen.

DECEMBER 25TH

CHRISTMAS DAY

2 PETER 1:2

MAY GRACE AND PEACE BE YOURS IN ABUNDANCE.
IN THE KNOWLEDGE OF GOD AND JESUS OUR Lord.

REJOICE! IT IS CHRISTMAS DAY, and our hearts are full. The joyful squeals, the grateful smiles, and the loving glances fill us with the fruition of the Advent season. Yes, the anticipation of Advent is over. Wait…is it?

May grace and peace be yours in abundance, is a wish of an immense measure of God's favor and peace.

And the true way to that peace is through our continuing faith and trust in him and our Lord Jesus.

In the knowledge of God and Jesus, our Lord. This isn't an ordinary blessing, rather encouraging words for our steadfast growth in our knowledge of God and Jesus, so the understanding of his grace and peace expands throughout our life.

May the love and grace of God and Jesus bless you this Christmas day and every other day. *But Mary treasured all these things and pondered them in her heart* (Luke 2:19). My wish is that we all continue to ponder these things in our hearts, hold them close, and treasure them forever.

Happy birthday, dear Jesus!

A Closing Reflection

The lilac bush is barren now. The branches covered in snow and ice. Its purple cones and glorious scent are but a mere memory.

Outside my window, the chickadees gather in the sinewy branches, waiting for their chance at the feeder.

Their carol is an ode to God. Trusting and glorifying in his faithful provisions.

I watch from my window and find such joy in the tiny birds.

They are filled with faithful bliss in God's blessings and his constant protection.

They fly on fearless wings into the cold winter wind.

I wonder where do they go when the day fades away into night?

God leads them to warmth and safety among the pines, and in the morning as the snow falls from the heavens, the chickadees return to my feeder.

What a beautiful gift they are. A reminder of the Father's steadfast love.

C.S. McDonald

CLOSING PRAYER

Dear Heavenly Father, as we extinguish the Advent candles, we give you thanks and praise for the glorious season of Advent. Let the glow of your everlasting love burn in our hearts and guide us through the upcoming year.

Help us to keep Jesus close, to walk and talk with him. May the Holy Spirit surround us and guide us along our faith journey.

Stir up the memory of Advent in our hearts to strengthen our faith and deepen our understanding as we anticipate our Savior's return.

In Jesus's victorious name.

Amen.

About C.S. McDonald

For twenty-six years, C.S. McDonald's life whirled around a song and a dance. She was a professional dancer and choreographer, educated through Pittsburgh Ballet School, Pittsburgh Dance Alloy, and many others. Starting in 1985, Cindy owned and operated a dance school, choreographed many musicals, and an opera for the Pittsburgh Savoyards. In 2011, she retired from her dance career to write. Under her real name, Cindy McDonald, she has penned murder suspense and romantic suspense novels. In 2014, she added the pseudonym, C.S. McDonald, to write the George the Pony children's books for her young grandchildren. When 2016 rolled around, Cindy began a new venture in writing mysteries—enter the Fiona Quinn Mysteries, a popular, best-selling cozy mystery series. In 2019, the Owl's Nest Mysteries, a time travel mystery series, debuted. All of her mysteries are clean-reads and based in her beloved hometown of Pittsburgh, Pennsylvania.

So, how does a mystery writer create a devotional? Well, as an active member of her church, Cindy attended the yearly Good Friday prayer vigil at her Lutheran Church. During the vigil, she was inspired to write a devotional book, and through much self-reflection and extensive prayer, she decided to start with an Advent devotional. Prayers for guidance were a huge part of the writing of this devotional.

Cindy and her husband, Bill, reside on their Thoroughbred farm known as Fly By Night Stables, accompanied by her Cocker Spaniel, Allister, and her Cavalier King Charles Spaniel, Charlie.

Thank you to these lovely services:

Cover design: DusktilDawn Designs
Editing: Silver Lining Editing Services
Formatting: Kathleen Harryman Digital Artist

For more books and information, please visit the C.S. McDonald Amazon author page:
C.S. McDonald Author Page

Made in United States
North Haven, CT
18 November 2025

82596931R00075